Measures and Handling Data

Activities for children with mathematical learning difficulties

Mel Lever

 David Fulton Publishers

David Fulton Publishers
2 Park Square, Milton Park, Abingdon, Oxon OX14 4RN

270 Madison Avenue, New York, NY 10016

First published in 2003
Transferred to digital printing

David Fulton Publishers is an imprint of the Taylor & Francis Group, an informa business

British Library Cataloguing in Publication Data
A catalogue record for this book is available from the British Library.

ISBN 1-85346-950-5

Designed and typeset by Kenneth Burnley, Wirral, Cheshire

Contents

Foreword

Mel Lever is an inspirational teacher of mathematics because she can teach maths to children who don't understand it and don't like it. She contrasts with other gifted maths teachers who can teach maths to children who are good at it. Since there seem to be more pupils who find maths challenging, Mel's ability to break concepts down and to find a creative way of making them accessible is of huge importance.

Mel teaches at Fairley House School, a specialist school for pupils with specific learning difficulties. She teaches maths on a daily basis and, as Maths and Key Stage 2 Coordinator, offers advice and ideas to colleagues. She is also someone who continues to learn and is always ready to take on board new ideas offered by others. She gives workshops to parents on helping children to overcome mathematical difficulties and is in great demand on the lecture circuit for teachers. This set of books means that a wider audience of parents and teachers can be inspired by her ideas.

Mel has studied the teaching of maths for many years and is very familiar with research in the area, particularly into mathematical difficulties. However, she has always chosen to go beyond the theory and to address the vital question: 'So what shall we do about it?' This is what makes her books so helpful; they give parents and teachers practical ideas they can use. Mel addresses the question of the types of difficulty encountered, then moves on to overcoming the difficulty.

At a recent maths workshop for governors, a governor commented, 'I wish Mel had taught me maths when I was at school'. I can only echo that sentiment and urge the reader of these books to enjoy learning from Mel how to teach maths to children who struggle and lag behind.

Jackie Murray
Principal and Educational Psychologist
Fairley House School

Introduction to the Series

Introduction

There are many children who, despite dedicated teachers, the introduction of the National Numeracy Strategy, wonderful books, and an abundance of maths equipment, still do not enjoy or understand mathematics.

We should focus on the two words 'enjoy' and 'understand' because I feel that unless children enjoy their maths, they are unlikely to fully understand it. Children may appear to be functioning reasonably and be achieving set goals, but I am sure that many children could achieve more if they had a 'fun time' with their maths.

I teach dyslexic and dyspraxic children at Fairley House School in London, many of whom have difficulties in understanding maths concepts and functioning mathematically. Over the years I have had to develop ways of interesting these children and helping them to learn. I have diagnosed their difficulties and set about changing my teaching, and that of others, so that maths could be presented to the children in a meaningful and fun way.

It is worth looking at the field of dyslexia in order to summarise the many ways in which children find learning difficult.

The British Dyslexia Association lists many factors that indicate dyslexia. I have picked out the following as being particularly relevant when trying to understand the mathematical learning difficulties of our children:

- Shows confusion between direction words, e.g. up/down, in/out.
- Has difficulty with sequence, e.g. coloured bead sequence, and, later, days of the week.
- Has inability to remember the label for known objects, e.g. 'table', 'chair'.
- Has difficulty learning nursery rhymes and rhyming words, e.g. 'cat', 'mat', 'sat'.
- Has particular difficulty with reading and spelling.
- Puts letters and figures the wrong way round.
- Has difficulty remembering tables, alphabet, formulae, etc.
- Still occasionally confuses 'b' and 'd' and words such as 'no/on'.
- Still needs to use fingers or marks on paper to make simple calculations.
- Has poor concentration.
- Has problems processing language at speed.
- Has difficulty telling left from right, order of days of the week, months of the year, etc.
- Has poor sense of direction.

Other relevant points could be added to this list. Many children with dyslexia have difficulty with left and right orientation. Many young dyslexic children need aids for doing any arithmetical computation. Some relinquish these aids at the same developmental stage as would the average child. However, the dyslexic and dyspraxic child may well need these aids for a longer time.

Difficulties in recalling multiplication tables are caused by short-term memory problems and by the inability to easily recognise sequences and patterns, thus removing props that help when memory fails. This leads to difficulties with working at speed to solve mathematical problems or when memorising, not only multiplication facts, but also addition, subtraction and division facts. It also leads to difficulties with telling the time, remembering the days of the week and months of the year.

I can hear many teachers and parents saying, 'My child has some of these problems, but he is not dyslexic. Why concentrate on dyslexia?' The simple answer is that I am not concentrating on dyslexia. I am hoping that, by outlining the above, I will give the reader an idea of the issues I am faced with in my work with dyslexic children. Many children have mathematical learning difficulties for a variety of reasons. Because I have worked with children who have difficulties in many areas of the curriculum and in all areas of mathematics, I have been forced to think of ways to overcome these difficulties. In doing so, I have found ways of interesting all children: the devices, games and methods I have developed have been of interest to children in general and their teachers.

Teachers of maths to children with mathematical learning difficulties are aware that every statement or teaching point needs to be rephrased and produced in a variety of ways, using concrete and pictorial methods, if the child is to make any sense of it. Asking a child to accept a mathematical fact and use it is not always helpful. The child may lack reference points and be unable to latch on to any signpost; he or she may lack any internal visual stimulus.

Teachers are constantly diagnosing the learning of their pupils; they learn how to adapt their teaching in the light of knowledge gained. Thus teachers are instruments of change in a school setting and thence in the wider world. Each teacher has a unique view of the wider educational community in which he or she is involved.

My teaching experience has led to a conviction that much mathematical learning is inhibited through children not being offered a wide enough mathematical vocabulary. This does not mean always *adding words* to the vocabulary; it might often mean *adding meaning* to the words already used by the children.

How the series is organised

The National Numeracy Strategy and Maths Schemes are mostly arranged in the expectation of an ordered, sequential and predictable path of learning. Teachers know that this is not how children learn. Maths is not a narrow subject; it is not just a series of truisms and facts. Maths is about discovery and logic; it is about pattern and shape; it is about order and chaos. Anyone reading that last sentence will have a different view of its meaning. We all have a different way of seeing and understanding the various aspects of mathematics. Some aspects of maths are easy for us to understand, some are not.

I considered arranging this series of books into year order: Years 1 to 6 or 7. I then realised that it is impossible to categorise need in this way. The activities I am suggesting are suitable for children in all these years. The principles concerned are adaptable. There is no lower or upper age limit to their usefulness and interest.

I decided to produce a series of books covering the various aspects of mathematics as followed in schools: number, shape and space, measures and handling data. I have omitted solving problems as a heading as this does not lend itself to a separate section here.

The books give ideas for activities to help children learn. Some ideas are more desk-bound than others. Many ideas involve children moving around. I suggest materials that teachers can produce, and supply photocopiable resources. There is much of the Numeracy Strategy that is not mentioned in these books. I have concentrated on areas where we have found children in need of a more creative approach. The creativity of early years teaching is not in question. I have been involved in bringing more creativity into the teaching of children in Years 3 to 6 especially.

Many of my colleagues also develop material for their maths classes and have been happy to contribute their ideas. Teachers are constantly on the look-out for ideas to help their children learn. Most are generous with sharing their ideas. I hope that this is another forum for discussion and that we shall all learn together.

Measures and Data Handling

I have put these two headings together as they both involve a lot of practical work and much of my work is similar to that done in all schools. Most of the activities that teachers and parents introduce to children help them learn in a way that is dependent on the child taking an active role in his or her own learning.

I have tried to expand the experience of the children, find ways to grab their imagination and make them want to take part and learn, and come back happily for more. I hope that teachers will find some new ideas that they can try with their children. I hope too that teachers and parents will give children time to do all the very practical activities that go with these aspects of maths. The tendency is for some teachers of children with mathematical learning difficulties to concentrate on number at the expense of some of these activities.

It is important that children experience opportunities in all aspects of maths. These aspects do not stand alone; all are interdependent. Give the children the experiences they deserve and their knowledge will grow throughout the various strands.

Acknowledgements

I would like to thank my colleagues at Fairley House for their help with getting this series together. In particular I would like to thank:

- Elizabeth Morrell for her support in setting up the project and for reading through the final draft;
- Jackie Murray for proof reading and giving helpful suggestions for improvement; and
- the following for allowing me to include their ideas:

    Mark Bolton
    Caroline Lillywhite
    Rosena Mentior
    Iona Mitchell
    Denise Mulholland
    Ann Osborn
    Jeanette Platt
    Joanne Tarr
    Veronica Woolvett

James Bentall helping with copying the photographs.

Measures

1 Teaching 'Time' to Children with Mathematical Learning Difficulties

I am starting this section with 'Time' as this is a most crucial concept for children to grasp if they are to become independent. During the past few years I have developed ways of helping the dyslexic children I teach, and other children I have taught in holiday projects, to understand the concept of time. I have invented games (some of which I am sure have already been thought of by others) and tried to ensure that the children have fun while learning.

Rote learning of the sequences of months of the year and days of the week can help children to memorise these facts, but the dyslexic child, or child with mathematical learning difficulties, may well need to practise these sequences more often than the average child.

As well as being able to tell the time from a clock face, children need to understand the *passage* of time, of months and days, of hours and minutes. Questions such as, 'If today is Tuesday, what day will it be in four days' time?' or 'If today is 29 December, what date will it be in one week's time?' are frequently asked in maths books and in tests. I noticed that, very often, many of the dyslexic children I teach would be able to answer the first of these questions, but few would be able to answer the second. There are several facts that children need to understand about the passage of a year if they are to understand such questions. I set about devising a set of activities which I hoped would help them to gain this understanding, and to do so in an active, fun way.

We talked about the scientific facts, and the children appeared to have little difficulty with understanding why we have years. We discussed how the days of the months arose, and the lengths of each month. So far, so good. However, they found it very difficult to understand *how* one month followed on from the next. Looking at a list of names was not sufficient. A diary shows details of the months but they are set out separately; they do not appear to run on from one to the other. What happens at the end of each month or the end of each year?

2 | The Passage of Time: Moving Through the Months

Activity

► Type out the months of the year and stick them on to strips of card, which you then laminate. Make a circle of 12 chairs, each facing outwards. Place the months clockwise on the chairs in the correct yearly order (Figure 2.1). In turn ask each child to walk round the chairs, starting with January, reciting the months as they go. Repeat this exercise, this time walking round twice. Then ask, 'What month comes after December?' Any child who is hesitant can check the answer by referring to the chair labels.

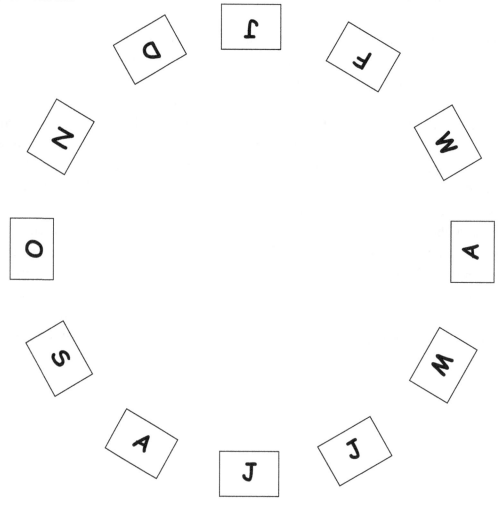

Figure 2.1

▶ Ask each child, in turn, to stand by his or her birthday month. Then ask what month it would be, say, three months later. The children walk round the chairs, counting the months. Do this several times, so that all children have a chance to cross the boundary from December to January.

▶ It is important that the children demonstrate the passage of time, so ask them to walk through one year, then one year and three months, then two years and two months, and so on. As the children become more involved in the activity they begin to enjoy moving as quickly as they can. You can ask them to demonstrate the passage of time in, say, five years and six months. Children then give each other instructions, with a maximum number of years allowed being ten. Running is allowed. Needless to say, after several minutes of this they are all rather exhausted!

▶ Ask if there is any way that they could find which month they would be in after two years, which did not involve running round the chairs. Someone will eventually tell you that if he or she started at March and walked through three years he or she would be back at March. Other children can give similar examples.

▶ Ask the children where they would be if they started at June and walked through 20 years, 100 years, 1,000 years. Continue with 20 years and 2 months, 100 years and 3 months and 1,000 years and 6 months. The children can stand at the given month and either count through the years, marching on the spot, or saying, 'After 20 years I would be at June and then after two months I would be at [walking on] July, August.'

▶ Repeat the above activities with seven chairs and the days of the week. The concept is the same.

It is a good idea to start with the larger concept of months first. Children can then go on to study a calendar and see where weeks fit into months.

RESOURCES

• Twelve chairs
• Names of the months on laminated cards

3 The Passage of Time: How Months Follow On

Many of my pupils had difficulty in answering questions such as, 'Look at a calendar. If today is 26 January, what date will it be in one week?' Virtually all the children I taught would say, 'How do I know? It doesn't say.' Given a page of a diary, they would point to the gap at the end of January. I decided, therefore, that if the children were to understand how one month followed another we would have to demonstrate this. The following activities help.

Activity

► Photocopy and enlarge the months from the front of a diary. Ask the children to cut out the names of the months and the dates of the months, keeping each name with its own set of dates (numbers). Keep the days of the week with January only. So, for instance, January and February might look like Figure 3.1 where February has only 28 days.

► Get the children to lay out the months on a piece of card, like a jigsaw, 1 February fitting into the gap next to 31 January, and so on. They should place the names of the months beside their dates as they go along. This is a time-

January / February – cut out these words and place next to the correct month

				1	2	3
4	5	6	7	8	9	10
11	12	13	14	15	16	17
18	19	20	21	22	23	24
25	26	27	28	29	30	31
1	2	3	4	5	6	7
8	9	10	11	12	13	14
15	16	17	18	19	20	21
22	23	24	25	26	27	28

Figure 3.1

consuming exercise, especially for children who have difficulty with fine motor skills, but this in itself helps to make it worth while. As they cut out the shapes the children have to concentrate hard not to cut off any dates and to keep the names of the months with their correct set of numbers. When they have finished laying out the year, they can stick it all together so that they have a calendar with no gaps.

(Dropping all the pieces on the floor is not a disaster! If this happens, pair children up to sort out the mess. They will soon find that each month has a unique shape, and by starting with January and fitting the other months in (taking account of the number of days in each month) it is possible to put the names on at the end.)

▶ Ask the children to highlight the 1st of each month. This makes it far easier for them to pick out each month and for them to refer to the calendar. An unbroken array of numbers is difficult for anyone to look at.

Having done this now with several groups of children, I have varied the instructions to suit the group. For instance, it may be that I ask the children to cut out one month and stick it on the card, lining up the name at the same time. With another group I might ask them to fit the dates together as they cut them out and then stick the names on at the end (thus helping them to practise saying the months in sequence).

These activities should generate a lot of discussion about how the months follow on from each other, and about the layout of calendars and diaries. When the children have their calendar strips they are able to answer questions such as:
'What is the date six weeks after 13 March?' or
'Point to 23 April. How many weeks and days is it to 23 July?'

The children can ask each other questions. They can work out how long it is between one child's birthday and another's.

It can be time-consuming and difficult to follow the activities above with a large class. If it is not appropriate to ask the children to cut out and stick together their own calendar, you can give them ready-cut-out pieces. Even if you ask the children to cut out their own calendars, it is always useful to make your own cut-out pieces (laminated, of course) for follow-up work (see Sheets A–C).

Photocopiable Sheets A to E show how the months can be fitted together. You need to photocopy them, cut out the dates of each month separately and then cut out the months of the year. You can leave the days of the week fixed to the top of January if you like.

This example could be called a Friday year, as it is the shape of a year that starts on a Friday. Other years start on other days. You could present this one to your children and ask if this is a calendar for the year you are in. Is it a leap-year calendar? What difference would there be if the calendar started on another day of the week? What difference would there be if it were a leap year?

This leads to further questions. 'Is your birthday on the same day each year? If not, why not?' 'How many days are there in a year? Check your answer on your calendar. Can you find a quick way of counting?' (Children can count in 7s or 14s. They can add the total for each month together.)

It is a simple step to ask them to find out how many days there are in each month. They are then helped to memorise these facts using their knuckles (Figure 3.2).

The months on the bumps (tops of knuckles) have 31 days. The months in the hollows have 30 days, except for February, which has 28, or 29 in a leap year.

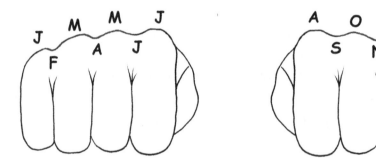

Figure 3.2

Following this they could count the weeks and days in each year. Many different methods can be used to do this.

I have found this an invaluable activity to do with my dyslexic children. I have also tried it with a group of children with mathematical learning difficulties, who had not been diagnosed dyslexic. They really enjoyed the activity and it was reported that they gained a lot of understanding through it.

Many children learn best through the use of concrete materials and 'manipulatives'. What better, or more fun way can you think of, to show how months follow on from each other, indeed flow in to each other? The children are not just manipulating their paper and scissors; they are manipulating their bodies – and enjoying it!

RESOURCES

- Laminated months that fit together
- Card
- Scissors
- Months from the front of a diary
- Glue
- Pens

				1	2	3	January							1
4	5	6	7	8	9	10	February	2	3	4	5	6	7	8
11	12	13	14	15	16	17	March	9	10	11	12	13	14	15
18	19	20	21	22	23	24	April	16	17	18	19	20	21	22
25	26	27	28	29	30	31	May	23	24	25	26	27	28	29
1	2	3	4	5	6	7	June	30	31	1	2	3	4	5
8	9	10	11	12	13	14	July	6	7	8	9	10	11	12
15	16	17	18	19	20	21	August	13	14	15	16	17	18	19
22	23	24	25	26	27	28	September	20	21	22	23	24	25	26
1	2	3	4	5	6	7	October	27	28	29	30	1	2	3
8	9	10	11	12	13	14	November	4	5	6	7	8	9	10
15	16	17	18	19	20	21	December	11	12	13	14	15	16	17
22	23	24	25	26	27	28		18	19	20	21	22	23	24
29	30	31	1	2	3	4		25	26	27	28	29	30	31
5	6	7	8	9	10	11		1	2	3	4	5	6	7
12	13	14	15	16	17	18		8	9	10	11	12	13	14
19	20	21	22	23	24	25		15	16	17	18	19	20	21
26	27	28	29	30	1	2		22	23	24	25	26	27	28
3	4	5	6	7	8	9		29	30	1	2	3	4	5
10	11	12	13	14	15	16		6	7	8	9	10	11	12
17	18	19	20	21	22	23		13	14	15	16	17	18	19
24	25	26	27	28	29	30		20	21	22	23	24	25	26
31	1	2	3	4	5	6		27	28	29	30	31		
7	8	9	10	11	12	13								
14	15	16	17	18	19	20								
21	22	23	24	25	26	27								
28	29	30	1	2	3	4								
5	6	7	8	9	10	11								
12	13	14	15	16	17	18								
19	20	21	22	23	24	25								
26	27	28	29	30	31									

M	T	W	T	F	S	S

Photocopiable Sheet A

M	T	W	T	F	S	S	
				1	2	3	January
4	5	6	7	8	9	10	
11	12	13	14	15	16	17	
18	19	20	21	22	23	24	
25	26	27	28	29	30	31	
1	2	3	4	5	6	7	February
8	9	10	11	12	13	14	
15	16	17	18	19	20	21	
22	23	24	25	26	27	28	
1	2	3	4	5	6	7	March
8	9	10	11	12	13	14	
15	16	17	18	19	20	21	
22	23	24	25	26	27	28	
29	30	31					

			1	2	3	4
5	6	7	8	9	10	11
12	13	14	15	16	17	18
19	20	21	22	23	24	25
26	27	28	29	30	**1**	2
3	4	5	6	7	8	9
10	11	12	13	14	15	16
17	18	19	20	21	22	23
24	25	26	27	28	29	30
31	**1**	2	3	4	5	6
7	8	9	10	11	12	13
14	15	16	17	18	19	20
21	22	23	24	25	26	27
28	29	30				

April

May

June

			1	2	3	4	July
5	6	7	8	9	10	11	
12	13	14	15	16	17	18	
19	20	21	22	23	24	25	
26	27	28	29	30	31	**1**	August
2	3	4	5	6	7	8	
9	10	11	12	13	14	15	
16	17	18	19	20	21	22	
23	24	25	26	27	28	29	
30	31	**1**	2	3	4	5	September
6	7	8	9	10	11	12	
13	14	15	16	17	18	19	
20	21	22	23	24	25	26	
27	28	29	30				

				1	2	3	October
4	5	6	7	8	9	10	
11	12	13	14	15	16	17	
18	19	20	21	22	23	24	
25	26	27	28	29	30	31	
1	2	3	4	5	6	7	November
8	9	10	11	12	13	14	
15	16	17	18	19	20	21	
22	23	24	25	26	27	28	
29	30	**1**	2	3	4	5	December
6	7	8	9	10	11	12	
13	14	15	16	17	18	19	
20	21	22	23	24	25	26	
27	28	29	30	31			

4 Telling the Time

Activity 1

Teachers can use the chair activity to demonstrate the movement of the fingers on a clock. The twelve hours are placed on a circle of chairs. One child is the hour hand and another the minute hand. They stand in the correct positions to demonstrate twelve o'clock. They are then asked to stand in the correct positions to demonstrate half-past twelve, quarter to one, one o'clock. Again this activity can have endless variations. (Teachers could cut out an hour hand and a minute hand of the appropriate length, and ask the children to place them in the correct positions.)

A geared teaching clock should be used to demonstrate how the two hands move at different speeds. This gives the opportunity to revise or discuss the time facts relating to seconds, minutes and hours. Children's geared clocks are available. These should always be used by children as they demonstrate the relative speeds of the fingers on the clock, when used properly.

Activity 2

To teach the 24-hour clock, place the numbers 1 to 12 in a circle on the floor and add the names of the hours beyond 12; 13 is placed on the outside of the circle next to 1, 14 next to 2, and so on.

▶ Ask two children, representing the hour hand and the minute hand, to stand at 12/24. They are both at midnight. Ask them to move to one o'clock in the morning, and demonstrate on a chart that this is written as 01.00. These four digits tell us that this is one o'clock in the morning. Now ask the children to walk through an hour as before, and illustrate this as 02.00.

▶ Ask two other children, again representing the hour hand and the minute hand, to stand at 11.00 (eleven o'clock in the morning). Ask them to walk through one hour to 12.00 (twelve mid-day). Tell the children that the day has now gone through twelve hours. If another hour passes, how many hours has the day gone through? Agree that thirteen hours have passed. If the children then walk on one hour they will get to 01.00 and 13.00. Explain that we would read this as 01.00 in the morning and as 13.00 in the afternoon.

▶ Show the children copies of a train timetable. Choose one train and follow its progress, using the floor numbers as above. This time, the children will have experience of part hours, still using the 24-hour clock. For instance, twenty past seven will be read as 07.20 in the morning, and as 19.20 in the evening.

▶ Ask the children if they can explain to each other how the numbers of the hours after mid-day can be quickly translated to the twelve-hour clock. Help them to see that three o'clock in the afternoon is 15.00, because twelve add three is fifteen.

This activity can generate a lot of discussion. How can the children explain 24.00 and 00.00? Does the latter make sense?

RESOURCES

- Twelve chairs
- Numbers 0 to 24
- Hour and minutes hands to fit the floor clock
- Geared teaching clock
- Copies of train timetable

5 | Capacity

All schools teach children volume and capacity through practical experience. With our children, who find it difficult to retain the meaning of terms, it is even more important that they are given enough meaningful experience to help them grasp the concepts as firmly as possible.

The following activities have proved useful.

Activity 1

Have a picnic with some of the dolls and teddies in the classroom. Fill two differently shaped 1-litre bottles with water (or orange). Give each doll one cup and ask the children how many cups they can fill out of the first bottle. Can they guess how many? When they have guessed, they can pour out the water. Give the dolls another set of cups. How many cups can the children fill out of the second bottle? They first guess and then pour out the water. They should be able to fill equal numbers of cups from each of the bottles. Ask them what this means. Point out the 'litre' word on the bottles. What does this tell us? Can they find other containers that can contain a litre? How many different shapes can they find? How do we measure litres?

Activity 2

Collect a variety of differently shaped and sized bottles and ask the children to put them in order, from the one that could contain the least amount of water to the one that could contain the most. Ask them to explain the order they have put the bottles in. Fill the first bottle with water. If they pour this into the second bottle, will it fill it? Will there be too much? These questions ensure that the children think again about what they have done with their ordering. If the first bottle contains the least amount of water, then it should not fill the second bottle. Experiment in this way and the children will gain the idea that liquid spreads out to fill the space provided and that they have to look at containers in a three-dimensional way to gauge how much they can hold.

Activity 3

Find a collection of bottles of different shapes and different sizes, with a 1-litre bottle being the largest. Fill them with water. Ask the children to estimate how much each contains. Show them a measuring jug marked in millilitres. Ask them what they think the markings show. Ask them to estimate the amount each bottle contains. Check the answers by measuring the water from each container in the measuring jug.

Activity 4

Discuss the language of capacity and use cubic containers to illustrate that volume and capacity are calculated by multiplying height × width × depth. Further illustrate this by drawing a rectangle measuring 5 cm by 4 cm on squared paper and working out the area. Then place one layer of cubic centimetre blocks on the shape and work out how many of these are needed to cover the shape. Using the formula work out, first the area (5 cm × 4 cm = 20 cm²). Then work out the volume (5 cm × 4 cm × 1 cm = 20 cm³). Why does 20 appear each time in the answer? Now add another layer of cubes and work out the volume again (5 cm × 4 cm × 2 cm = 40 cm³). What do you notice about the volume the first time and the volume the second time?

Activity 5

If you are having a Christmas Fair, do a project with the older children, asking them to work out how many bottles of wine are needed for the mulled wine. They will need to work out the capacity of the cups being used and the amount of wine in each bottle.

Activity 6

Staffrooms often end up with too much milk. One group of children could work out how much milk is needed per day. They need to construct a questionnaire asking each teacher:

- 'How many cups of tea or coffee do you have in a day?'
- 'Do you drink them white or black?'
- 'Can you indicate on this plastic cup the amount of milk you put in your cup?'
- 'Do you ever drink milk on its own?'
- 'Do you have milk with cereal?'

Armed with this information the children can do a very practical task of working out how much milk is needed, on average, each day.

RESOURCES

- Dolls and teddies
- Plastic containers in a variety of shapes and sizes
- Measuring bottles, jugs and flasks
- Cups
- Centimetre cubes
- Squared paper
- Pencils

6 | Cooking

This is a favourite practical activity for many teachers. It is a very important activity for children who find maths difficult to understand. For the very young ones it is an everyday activity, which has a great ending – they get to eat the food! For older children it helps them see that maths is part of everyday life.

The following are activities that are easy to prepare. Remember that the questions are a very important part of the activity.

Activity 1

Choose one potato for each child and ask each child to weigh his or her potato. Peel the potatoes and weigh again. How much weight has each one lost? Do the same with a carrot each. Compare the weight of the carrot and the potato. Which is the heaviest? Which is the lightest? Weigh all the vegetables together. Can the children estimate the total weight? Make a litre of stock, using a stock cube. Take the opportunity to pour it into different containers so that the children can see that the quantity remains the same even though the liquid fills a different shaped space. Boil and simmer your vegetables in the stock until they are soft. Liquidise the mixture. Ask the children to think about how much their vegetables weighed at the beginning. How much do they think the stock weighed? (You can, if you like, weigh the stock before you begin.) Weigh the finished 'stew' or 'soup'. What weight do we have now? Is it the same as when we started? If so, why? If not, why not?

Activity 2

Make a ginger biscuit mixture. Weigh it. Divide it up so that each child has the same quantity. Ask them to make a gingerbread figure. Put two (or more) buttons on each figure. Cook the biscuits. Line the figures up. Ask questions, for instance:

- How much does each gingerbread figure weigh?
- How much do they weigh altogether?
- If you sold them at 10p each, how much would you get?
- How many buttons do they have altogether?
- How many buttons do five (six, seven . . .) figures have?

Activity 3

Buy a pizza base for each child. Give each child a tomato, a piece of cheese and a small cooked sausage. Ask them to weigh each item and then find the total. Check by weighing them all together. Slice the tomato and lay on the base, cover with the sliced cheese and sliced sausage. Cook for the required time. Weigh again. Ask questions, for instance:

* How much does each pizza weigh?
* Is the cooked weight the same as the weight before cooking? (If not, why not?)
* How much do they weigh altogether?
* If you sold them at 50p each, how much would you get?
* If you cut them in half, how many people could share them?
* If you cut them in quarters, how many people could share them?

Activity 4

Find a basic recipe book. Plan a meal for two people. Choose the items and calculate how much they would weigh. For instance, chicken breast could be 200 g, you might need half a kilo of potatoes for two people, and so on. The important thing in this exercise is the discussion that goes on before, the research that can be done at home and the actual weighing and cooking, which will generate questions such as the above.

You can always bring money into these activities. Older children need to be thinking of value for money, and the relative cost of different meals. You can use publicity from shops and the Internet to find the cost of the items you are choosing.

Use a variety of types of balance. You can use kitchen scales, scales with weights and balances (for comparison). Be inventive.

RESOURCES

* Food
* Knives and spoons, potato peeler
* Cutting boards and other appropriate kitchen utensils
* Measuring jugs and other containers
* A variety of scales
* Recipe book
* Lists of prices

7 How Heavy Are You?

It is amazing how many children do not know the answer to this, or know their weight in stones only. I find that when starting to discuss weight with our Year 3 or 4 children it is necessary to begin with this very practical question. They will have learned about weight and mass earlier, but children with learning difficulties tend to forget such facts and need encouragement to recall previous learning.

Activity

Explain that weight is measured in grams and kilograms. Show the children a gram and a kilogram weight. Ask each child to hold a 1 g weight and a 1 kg weight. How many grams do they think they will need to make 1 kg? Discuss their estimations.

▶ When they have offered all their (fairly wild) suggestions you can tell them that there are 1,000 grams in 1 kilogram. Ask what items they think are measured in grams and what in kilos. It is useful to refer to items bought in the supermarket and at the chemist: apples are weighed in kilos; sliced meat is weighed in grams. Have some packets or labels to show them. Show them supermarket publicity, which gives pictures of items and their prices per unit.

▶ Ask the children to work in groups to estimate the weight of small objects and check them on a balance with 1 g weights. They should keep a record of their estimates and the actual weights. Each group then compares results. Did they all get better at estimating? Which group was better at estimating?

▶ Give each group some 1 kg weights. Ask them to hold one weight, then two and as many as they can. This usually results in some macho posturing! Can each group find an item that they think weighs one kilogram? Exchange items with those of another group. Are both right?

▶ How many kilograms do the children think they weigh? You need a grid as in Figure 7.1. (See p. 23 for a photocopiable grid.)

▶ In the first column write the names or initials of all the children who volunteer to be weighed. (Remember, some children are self-conscious about their weight and they must be given a choice as to whether or not they want to be weighed.) In the next column write their estimation of their weight. Ask them to write it on a piece of paper first and then fold this over. They then open their paper one by one and

Name	Estimated weight 1	Estimated weight 2	Actual weight	Difference

Figure 7.1

read out their estimation, checked by a partner to ensure that they are not influenced by a previous estimate. For the second estimation, weigh one child on scales and write down his or her actual weight. Ask the children to revise their first estimates if they want to and put these in the third column. For the fourth column weigh all the children. Write in their actual weights. For the last column you can ask the children to find the difference between their first estimation and their actual weight, or the second estimation and their actual weight – or both.

▶ As a follow-up to the above activity, measure the heights of the children and construct a graph to show heights and weights. Discuss this graph.

RESOURCES

- Gram and kilogram weights
- Packets
- Labels
- Supermarket publicity
- Weight chart
- Paper
- Pencils
- Scales

How Heavy Are You?

Name	Estimated weight 1	Estimated weight 2	Actual weight	Difference

Photocopiable Sheet F

8 Measuring Your Body

Many teachers get children to measure themselves in the early years in school. For children with learning difficulties this is even more important as these children often have difficulty in understanding relative sizes, where they fit in, in the overall picture, and in retaining facts relating to their size and the size of common items in their world.

A colleague who was teaching Year 3 children decided to ask the children to measure themselves. She made sure that their activities encompassed as many mathematical concepts as possible.

Activity 1

▶ Draw round head and neck and cut out.

▶ Measure shoulders and cut out length of paper to match. Roll paper to make a cylinder.

▶ Measure trunk from neck to seat and make another cylinder.

▶ Measure arms to wrist and make cylinders.

▶ Draw round hands and cut out.

▶ Measure legs to ankle and make cylinders.

▶ Draw round feet and cut out.

▶ Put the body together with tape and then measure to find out the height of the model. Compare this with the height of the actual child measured against the wall or door. Are the measurements the same? If so, why? If not, why not? The probability is that the measurements will not match. This will engender much discussion about why this is so.

A lot of mathematical and natural language is used in this exercise. Make a list of the words used and then come back later and ask the children to define the terms. (Language used will include: length, height, metre, centimetre, cylinder.)

RESOURCES

- Tape measures
- Sugar paper
- Newspaper
- Compasses
- Card
- Sticky tape
- Scissors
- Rulers
- Buttons
- Glue

Activity 2

Give the children dimensions of an animal. The best ones to try are a cat and a rabbit. Show a picture of the chosen animal so that the children can orientate it correctly. Instructions for a cat could be:

▶ Draw a circle which measures 10 cm across. This is called the diameter of the circle. Cut it out. This is the cat's head.

▶ Draw a circle 30 cm across (diameter) and cut this out.

▶ Draw two triangles with sides measuring 4 cm. These triangles are called equilateral triangles.

▶ Draw four rectangles, the sides of each one measuring 30 cm along the long sides, and 3 cm along the short sides.

▶ Design your own paws. Use buttons for eyes.

▶ Put together as shown in Figure 8.1:

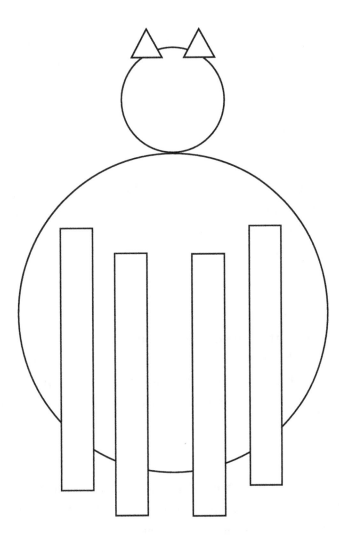

Figure 8.1

9 Measuring Length: Non-standard Units

Most children understand the idea of length but have difficulty with remembering the terminology, with comparing lengths, estimating and finding the shortest, most efficient way of finding a length. The following suggestions build up from early experiences to later ones, although many children do not learn in a predicted sequence.

Activity 1

Compare heights. Stand two children back to back and ask who is the taller and who is the shorter. Can anyone think of something that they could stand on the head of the shorter child to make him or her the same height as the taller? Write up and display the key words.

Activity 2

Make some cut-out people of different heights. Pin them to the wall or lay them on the floor along a straight line. Do the above activity and see if the children can come up with a variety of items to fill in the gaps. This time you can introduce the words 'shortest' and 'tallest'. Write them and display them.

Activity 3

Ask the children to draw their own large people. How tall are they? What can they measure with? Give the children a variety of objects, such as straws, plastic cups, Multilink. If they all choose a different object, ask how they can compare heights. This should lead them to see that they need to measure with the same units in order to compare.

Activity 4

Display a variety of items on a table. Ask the children to estimate how many cubes would be in a Multilink tower the same height as each object. They *must* estimate the answers, make the towers and then try out their towers. There is a prize for the best estimate.

Activity 5

Ask the children to estimate the length and width of a desk or a door. As a group they should decide what is the best way to give the answer, using non-standard units, e.g. in straws. Ask each one to estimate the number of straws needed to go along each side of the desk, or to reach to the top of the door.

Activity 6

Label various items in the hall A, B, C, D, E, F, G, etc. Label vertical and horizontal lengths. For instance, label a door and a line on the floor. Label the height and width of the piano. Label the width of the doorway. Ask the children to work in groups to decide, by sight and estimation alone, which of these measures the most, which the least and put the others in order, longest to shortest. They should write their results on a piece of paper. Groups then compare results. Give them some sheets of paper and ask how they can check their results. They should cut out strips and compare lengths. If they make strips the length or width required they could then lay them down to compare them. Stress the importance of a base line.

RESOURCES

- Paper
- Scissors
- Straws
- Plastic cups
- Multilink
- Labels

10 Measuring Length: Standard Units

To remember the terminology, the children need to discover its meaning for themselves. This is important for all children, but very important for children with learning difficulties. Avoid the temptation to give information instead of allowing time for the children to discover it!

Activity 1

Show the children a metre stick and ask how many items they can think of that have the same length or height as the stick. Design a poster giving this information. They can draw the objects, but must decide what length is going to represent a metre. This will be an introduction to scale drawing and can be mentioned without labouring the point. A good idea is to lead them to use 10 cm to represent 1 metre. Write down the words in bold above and display them.

Activity 2

Ask the children to write down or draw as many items as they can think of that are longer or taller than a metre. Then ask them to write down or draw items that are shorter than a metre. Discuss the language, write it down and display it.

Activity 3

Discuss the length of a metre stick and give them the information that 100 cm are equal to 1 m. Write this down and display it.

Activity 4

Ask them how many centimetres there are in half a metre. How many in quarter of a metre?

Activity 5

Put the children into small groups and ask them to choose one child to measure. They must use a tape measure to measure:

- the length and width of his head;
- the length of his neck;
- the length of his arms to the tip of his fingers;
- the length of his legs and, separately, his feet;
- the length of his torso;
- the width of his shoulders.

Take these measurements and cut strips of paper, 2 cm wide, to the lengths measured, plus 1cm. For the head draw an oval using the two measurements taken. Use butterfly pins to join the various bits together (this is why they needed the extra 1 cm). Lay their paper model down and measure it from the top of the head to the ends of its feet. Compare it with the live model. Note the children's use of language. (This activity is similar to the one described previously, but is a more accurate activity for more competent children.)

Activity 6

Make a collection of a variety of everyday items: an exercise book, a pencil, a tin, a box, a board marker, a photo and so on. Use as many as you can so that they do not become too familiar to the children too soon. You need some that are similar in size and some that are obviously different. This helps all children to have a result. Measure these items carefully, noting which dimension you are measuring, and mark the dimension with a strip of paper. Write the dimensions on pieces of card or laminated paper. Spread the items on the hall floor. Games that can be played with these include:

▶ Divide children into teams and label each child from A onwards. Give one dimension label to each A child and ask him or her to put this label on the item to which they think it belongs. Give them 10–20 seconds to decide (vary the time according to competence). The first child correct scores a point for his or her team. The team with the most points at the end wins.

▶ As above but give the children two (or more) labels at once.

▶ Starting with A from each team, give each child two cards with the same dimensions on them (but different from each other's). Give them 10–20 seconds to label two matching items.

Activity 7

Cut out strips of paper of varying lengths and widths. Make sure that some are the same length but a different width. Make dimension labels for each strip of paper. Lay the strips on the hall floor. Divide children into groups as above. Play the following games:

▶ Give one dimension label to each A child and ask him or her to put this label on the item to which they think it belongs. Give them 10–20 seconds to decide (vary the time according to ability). The first child correct scores a point for his team. The team with the most points at the end wins.

▶ As above but give the children two (or more) labels at once.

▶ Starting with A from each team, give each child two cards with the same dimensions on them (but different from each other's). Give them 10–20 seconds to label two matching items.

RESOURCES

- Metre stick
- Rulers
- Paper and pencils
- Tape measure
- Scissors
- Butterfly pins
- Everyday items
- Card
- Poster

11 | Measuring Lines: Standard Units

Children often find it difficult to use a ruler. They need to learn to hold it steadily, to find the beginning point when measuring (some rulers have a space before 0) and see the exact point where their measuring stops. Children who are dyspraxic find it very difficult to organise all this. Dyslexic children often forget the rules. They all need a lot of help and practice to be able to measure accurately.

Wooden rulers with no millimetres and blocks of colour are often difficult for children to use for measuring. They need experience with plastic rulers with sharp edges so that they can easily see over the edge, and with the numbers written on or below the lines. With some wooden rulers the number is written in the space, which is good for number line practice, but not easy for children to adapt to a measuring instrument.

Measuring lines

The following activities help children build up their expertise while having fun.

Activity 1

▶ Measure the lines on Photocopiable Sheet G. This sheet has a series of straight horizontal lines. This exercise helps the children to keep the ruler level.

▶ Make up other sheets like this and introduce a bit of competition. Who can be the first to get all measurements correct?

▶ Measure the lines on Photocopiable Sheet H. This sheet has a series of straight vertical lines. This exercise helps children to be more flexible in their use of a ruler. Expertise with this also helps children when ruling margins.

▶ Again, make up other sheets like this and introduce a bit of competition. Who can be the first to get all measurements correct?

▶ Measure the straight lines on the picture on Photocopiable Sheet I. This robot is also symmetrical; this gives teachers the opportunity to discuss symmetry. Do the children need to measure each line or can they predict the length of some?

▶ Measure the straight lines on the picture on Photocopiable Sheet J. This is not a symmetrical picture, but the children may find some short cuts.

Measure the lines using a ruler.
Write the measurements next to each line.

Measure the lines using a ruler.
Write the measurements next to each line.

Measure the robot using a ruler.
Write the measurements next to each line.

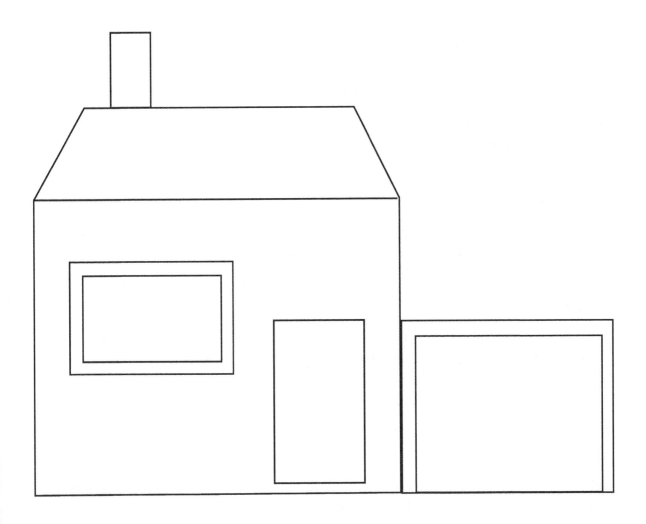

Photocopiable Sheet J

The discussion that arises when doing these activities is a very important part of the exercise. Children should be encouraged to discuss every aspect of the work and to compare their work with that of others. As a class, make a list of the difficulties that arose and how they could be avoided in future.

Take advantage of these activities to revise other concepts, such as symmetry, estimation, shape.

DRAWING LINES ACCURATELY

Drawing accurate lines is usually more difficult for children than measuring lines. These ideas reflect the activities above.

Activity 2

Ask children to draw straight horizontal lines on a sheet (see Photocopiable Sheet G). They should then swap their efforts with a friend and check each other's work.

Activity 3

Ask children to draw vertical lines on a sheet (see Photocopiable Sheet H). They should then swap their efforts with a friend and check each other's work.

Ask them to repeat these exercises as often as you like.

Activity 4

Ask children to draw a picture using straight lines. Use centimetre squared paper to help keep the lines straight. Make two photocopies of each picture. Ask them to write the measurements on the lines on one copy and ask a friend to measure the second. Check to see that they both have the same measurements.

Activity 5

Ask children to draw a symmetrical picture, using centimetre squared paper, and ask a friend to copy it.

SCALE

This is a really difficult concept for many children to grasp, but especially so for children with mathematical learning difficulties. It should be introduced in a very simple manner. These activities should help children.

Activity 6

Give children a drawing of a rectangular garden on a piece of centimetre squared paper. The longer side should measure 20 cm and the shorter 10 cm. It will need square and rectangular flowerbeds in it and a rectangular garden table. Keep lines drawn on the lines of the paper. Does this look like a plan of a garden? Is it the same size as an actual garden? (The discussion that ensues here gives teachers the opportunity to discuss the drawing of plans in general, the importance of accuracy and the question of scale.)

Activity 7

Explain that drawings and plans as used by architects and planners could not possibly be the actual size of the construction. Tell them that for your garden you have used 1 cm to represent 1 m. Ask the children to count or measure the dimensions of the drawing. Then ask them to say how many metres the actual garden would measure. Repeat this with the flowerbeds and table.

Activity 8

Ask the children to draw their own plan of a garden. It does not have to be rectangular, but it does need to be drawn with straight lines. Measure in centimetres and then translate to metres.

Activity 9

Choose one of the plans and use it to construct a garden plan to size. (You need to have checked the size of the drawing and the size of the school hall to do this!) Take a pile of newspaper into the hall and ask children to roll or fold newspaper to make strips. Use adhesive tape to secure the shape and to join strips. Using metre rules construct the garden plan by checking dimensions on the scale plan.

Activity 10

A greater challenge would be to ask the children to make a scale model of a room – possibly their classroom. This is a valuable way of getting the children to work together and to discuss their work as they go along. If children are given specific tasks, they soon learn the importance of being really accurate in order not to spoil the finished product. This exercise can overlap with work done in geography or DT.

A lot of work done on measuring is carried out in other lessons. It is important not to miss opportunities to extend the children's experience and language during these lessons. They need to be able to see and understand the connections between various aspects of the curriculum.

Do not forget the importance of clothes sizes. Children need to be aware of their own measurements and what the figures mean. They could compare prices of various items of different sizes. Are all children's clothes cheaper than adult clothes? This will be an interesting starter to a PSHE lesson.

RESOURCES

- Rulers
- Centimetre squared paper
- Paper
- Pencils
- Newspaper
- Sticky tape
- Metre rules

12 | Measuring a Greater Length: Non-standard and Standard Units

Estimation and reasoning continue to be central to the learning of our children. The following worked well with a group of Year 4 children, giving opportunities for cooperation, estimation, reasoning, using numeracy skills and extending language.

MEASURING THE HALL

Our hall is marked out for PE and games. The floor looks like Figure 12.1.

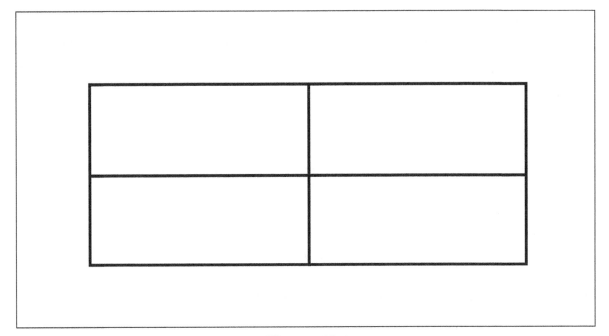

Figure 12.1

The outer line marks the walls of the hall. The darker lines represent the games markings.

The following ideas have been enjoyed by many children, who learn through movement, estimation, cooperation and discovery.

Activity

▶ Collect a variety of measuring instruments: metre sticks, tape measures, trundle wheels, rulers, string. Divide the children into four groups and allocate one small marked rectangle to each group.

▶ Ask each group to estimate the length and width of their small rectangle.

▶ Ask them to measure the sides, using any of the instruments they like, or a mixture, and give a total for the perimeter of their shape.

▶ Report on the results and compare how each group measured and if any groups had matching results. (Each rectangle is the same size.)

▶ Can anyone think of a quicker way of measuring their rectangle?

At this point you hope the children will notice that:

- opposite sides are of equal length;
- there is no need to measure each side separately;
- if they get four different measurements there must be a mistake;
- it is important to measure more than once to check results.

▶ Ask the children to measure again, changing the instruments they use, and see if they get the same result.

▶ Compare the results.

Eventually, each group should come up with the same set of measurements.

▶ Ask each group to write down the measurements they have taken. They should now work out how far they would walk if they:

- walked round the perimeter of the large rectangle;
- walked round the perimeter of a small rectangle.

▶ Compare results. How did they work this out? Note what rules of number each child used. How many of them multiplied?

▶ How many rectangles can they find in the whole shape?

▶ How many rectangles can they see in the hall?

▶ Why are there so many rectangles?

This latter discussion helps fix the event in the children's minds. They have had fun doing the exercise, used mathematical language, extended their thinking, worked co-operatively and used various aspects of mathematics. They are ready to think about area.

RESOURCES

- Metre sticks, trundle wheels
- Tape measures
- Rulers
- String
- Paper
- Pencils
- Words mounted on card to reinforce words used in lesson

13

Finding the Area: Non-standard and Standard Units

Having measured the length and width of the games markings in the hall, an opportunity arises to tackle area in a meaningful way.

Activity

▶ Sit the children round the outside of the shape and ask them if they can describe how big it is. They should reiterate the language used on the previous occasion.

▶ Explain that they have now given the size of the outside of various parts of the shape. We now want to find out how much space we have covered. Ask the children to discuss how they could explain this to someone else.

▶ Share suggestions. Lead the discussion to the need to describe the whole of the floor inside the lines. Explain the difference between the outside measurements and the surface measurements.

▶ How could we model the surface space? We could copy it and carry it away with us. Suggest we use newspaper to copy it. Give children piles of newspaper (either all tabloid or all broadsheet) and masking tape and ask them, in four groups, to copy the space of one of the smaller rectangles.

▶ Compare models. Have we all used the same amount of paper?

▶ Describe the models. They will have used a certain number of pages or double pages.

▶ Give out 1 cm squared paper and ask the children to draw a rectangle on it. Can they see any way of describing the space enclosed by the rectangle? Lead the children to count the number of squares inside the shape.

Explain that we can express this as so many square centimetres.

▶ Look at the floor. What could we do to describe the space contained by our rectangles? Eventually you will arrive at the need to use standard units.

▶ Ask the children to make square metres of paper, using sugar paper. This will be an arduous task, so have some ready for use! Lay these on a small rectangle. How many square metres did we use? Is there any way we could have known this before cutting out the squares?

▶ Does anyone know what we have been measuring? Initially we measured the perimeter of our shapes. Now we have been measuring the space enclosed by the perimeter. This is called the area. Ask the children to think of instances where they have heard this word used or where people have discussed square metres. Include your own ideas. Suggestions might be:

- The park covers a large area.
- What area of London do you come from?
- How much does that carpet cost for a square metre?
- Cleaning curtains is charged by the square metre.
- How much paint do I need to paint this room? Look at the tin to see how many square metres the paint will cover.

▶ Give each child a piece of 1 cm squared paper, with a variety of shapes drawn on it: square; rectangle; triangle; octagon. Make sure that you follow the lines on the paper as much as possible. Ask the children to work out how many squares are enclosed by each shape. They will have to count bits of squares to make whole ones. Compare answers. Which shapes were easier to deal with?

▶ Ask children to look at the rectangles and squares only. How did they calculate the number of squares inside each shape? Some children will have counted each square. Some will have realised that they have rows of squares repeated and could therefore count in 5s, 7s, or whatever the width of the shape is.

▶ Now you can introduce the standard formula: area = length × width. Help children to work out the area of the shape in the hall.

I have found that starting from large units, then introducing smaller ones and then returning to the larger ones works well for my children as they have been moving about and getting very involved in a practical way.

RESOURCES

- Newspaper
- Sugar paper
- Masking tape
- Centimetre squared paper
- Pencils
- Rulers
- Metre sticks

14 | Maths Competition

Ask each pupil in your class/group to estimate the area of the PE area in the hall. The answer should be in square metres. There will be a prize for the most accurate – as long as we are assured that there is no cheating. The space we are thinking of is marked like this:

Handling Data

15 | Sets and Sorting

It is very important that children with mathematical learning difficulties do not miss out this aspect of their learning. Due to the slowness with which they learn some concepts, there is a temptation for teachers to carry on to the next item. This may be done for the best of reasons. You hope that the child will eventually pick up the concepts as he or she watches others. There is a lot of other work to be done and you do not want the child to miss this too. However, mathematics centres on making the right decisions, seeing patterns and sequences, seeing similarities and differences, and thinking things through. These early activities help children to develop in all these areas.

In Years 1 and 2 children are asked to 'solve a given problem by sorting, classifying and organising information in simple ways . . .' (Numeracy Strategy). Teachers must be inventive in finding opportunities for older children to sort and organise. There are many everyday opportunities. They can:

- sort the pens and pencils;
- tidy and order the reading books;
- give out books and papers to the rest of the class;
- help to invent a recording system for borrowing class books;
- water plants at regular intervals;
- check that coats are on the correct pegs;
- match up scattered shoes and trainers.

There are endless possibilities. It is tempting to ask the most efficient children to help with classroom organisation. However, it is the child with learning difficulties who will gain most from it.

There are many products available for early sorting activities. With younger children it is useful to ask them to make items to be sorted. The following have proved to be popular.

Activity 1

Ask the children to make peg dolls. They can choose from three hair (wool) colours (brown, black, yellow), three felt colours to make dresses (blue, red, orange) and three eye colours (blue, brown, green). They can colour the ends of the peg to give their dolls some shoes, using felt tips with three colours to choose from (grey, pink, purple). Choosing a variety of colours helps the children to rehearse and revise colour names and teaches them to observe carefully. They can sort in one set, in two or in three. (See Figures 15.1 to 15.3.)

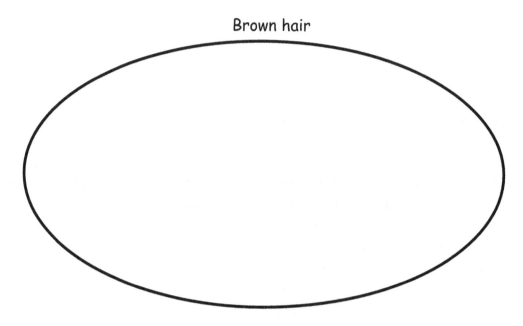

Figure 15.1

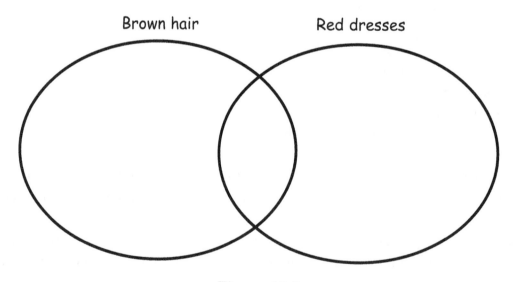

Figure 15.2

RESOURCES

- Wooden pegs
- Wool
- Felt
- Felt tips
- Scissors
- Sorting circles

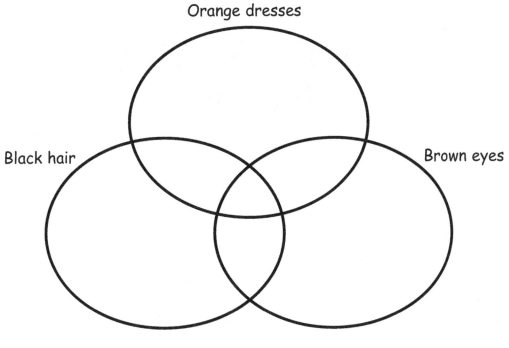

Figure 15.3

Activity 2

Make simple house pictures and ask the children to colour them. Restrict the number of colours they use. Use the results to sort in several categories. (See Figure 15.4.)

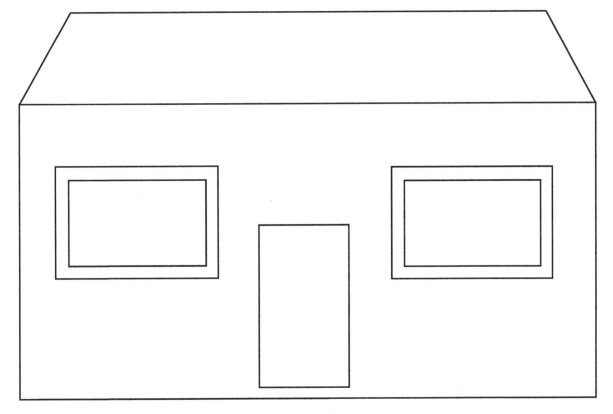

Figure 15.4

16 Sets and Sorting: Decision Trees

Many children with learning difficulties need help to make decisions. At home and school willing parents and teachers might have helped them. If children take time to come up with an answer there is often a peer nearby who will supply it. I think work on decision trees helps all children to think about their responsibilities in decision-making. It is especially helpful for the child who does not find learning easy.

Food is often a good way to fire a child's imagination. The following is from my Maths Diploma Course, which I started in 1986.

Attached are two examples of decision trees (Photocopiable Sheets K and L). You may think that a tree should be upright. However, it may seem to you more logical to move from left to right. You can use both examples with children, so that they can see that there are many ways to solve a problem.

- Write on the board a list of the items available at a hotel for breakfast: bacon, egg, sausage, tomato. (Everyone gets tea or coffee and toast.)
- Tell the children that you are going to find out how many different combinations of breakfast there are.
- Give the children ten minutes to see if they can come up with all the different variations. (Some will have done so, some will have missed out some choices, some will be logical, some will try out random selections, some will not know where to start.)
- Tell them that you are going to show them how to use a decision tree to help sort out problems like this.

Activity: What shall we have for breakfast?

▶ Explain that for every item you can either choose it or not.

▶ Give the children a decision tree each or one between two (using Photocopiable Sheet K).

▶ Explain that the first choice is whether to have bacon or not. Therefore, at the point where the branches start to go in two separate ways, you need to label one branch 'bacon' and one branch 'not bacon' (usually marked, as in Venn diagrams, as 'bacon' and 'bacon').

▶ Having chosen bacon you then need to choose to have or not have egg. You will then end up with your tree looking like Figure 16.1. Ask the children to read from the

50

bottom the choices they have made so far. The first choice is to have bacon and egg. The next one is to have bacon only. The third is to have egg only and the fourth is to have neither. Show the children a large version of the tree. (An OHP comes in handy here.)

▶ Ask the children to continue labelling their trees. Check when they have finished. The trees should look like Figure 16.2.

▶ Show the finished version and go over the choices and the pathways.

▶ Write out the various choices in order, using just initials to show a pattern, e.g.:

▶ Now ask the children to think of other common experiences where choices have to be made in this way. One might be choosing what types of flowers to have in a bouquet.

▶ Do similar exercises using Photocopiable Sheet L.

RESOURCES

- Decision trees
- OHP transparencies
- Pencils
- Paper

Decision Tree

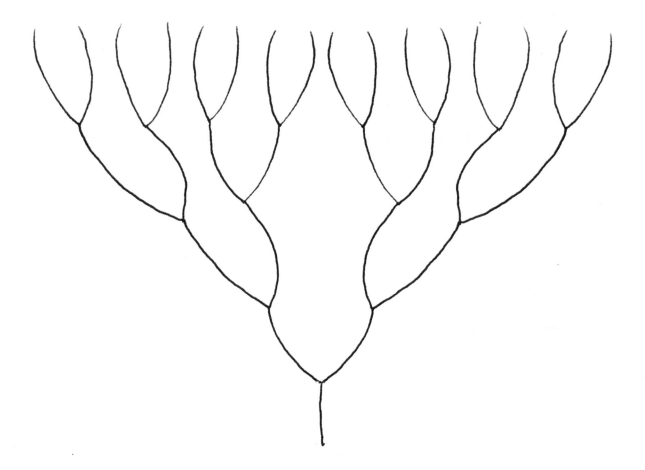

Decision Tree

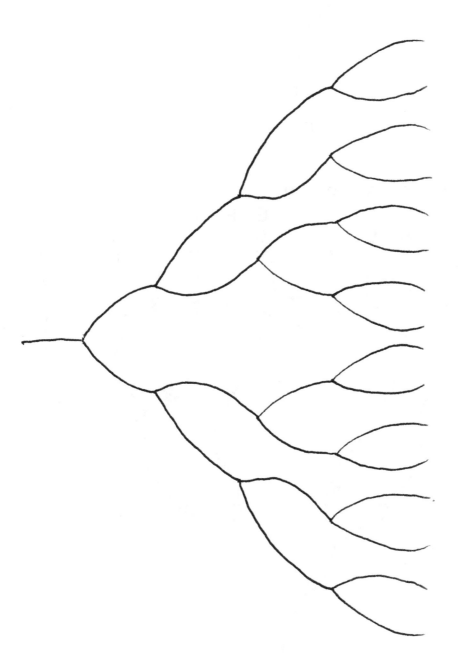

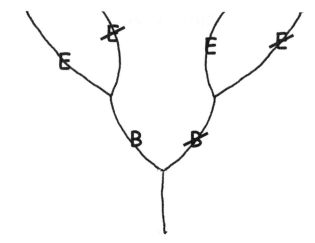

Figure 16.1

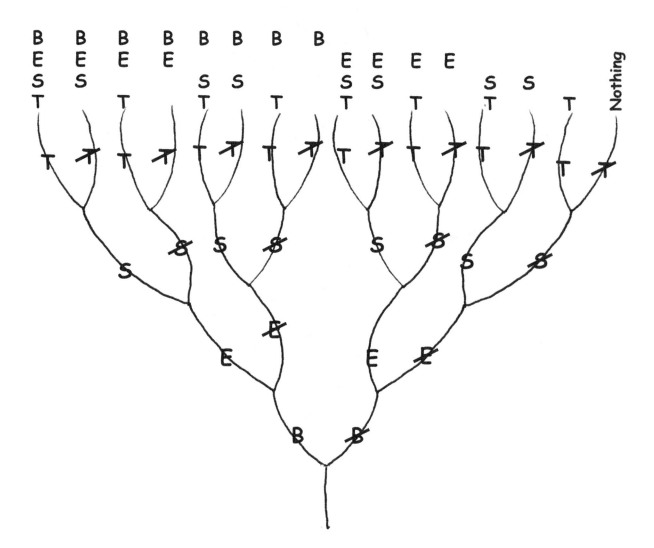

What do you want for breakfast? Choose between B, E, S and T.

Figure 16.2

17 | Interpreting Data

Many children with mathematical learning difficulties have problems with interpreting data. Sometimes it is the formality of the picture. Graphs look threatening to some children! They need help to read the graphs, to see that pictures and illustrations are ways of representing algebraic functions.

Children generally find the early activities in using graphs not too difficult to understand and use. The problems that some children have concern the language used and the need to use a scale which is uniform and easy to read.

Language which the children need to learn to use accurately includes: number, scale, count, axis, axes, how many/much, most, least, the same as, greatest, smallest, compare, how many/much more. The following ideas help children to succeed.

PICTOGRAMS

Activity 1

Present a simple pictogram and ask the children to interpret it. For example, using Figure 17.1, ask the following questions:

- How many frogs were near the tree?
- Which creature did the children find least of?
- Which creature did the children find most of?
- How many more frogs were found than butterflies?
- Can you say how many there were of each creature?
- Could we make our own bar chart? What could we record? (Possibilities could be pets owned by children in the class.) Discuss the need to have one standard picture or illustration.

Activity 2

Use Figure 17.2 to show the importance of reading the axis – in this case each symbol represents two units. Ask the following questions:

- How many of each creature were found?
- How many more frogs were found than butterflies?
- How many frogs were near the tree?
- Which creature did the children find least of?
- Which creature did the children find most of?
- The number of frogs found was the same as the number of which other creature?
- Compare the two charts (Figures 17.1 and 17.2). Compare the numbers of each creature found in the two charts. What do you notice?

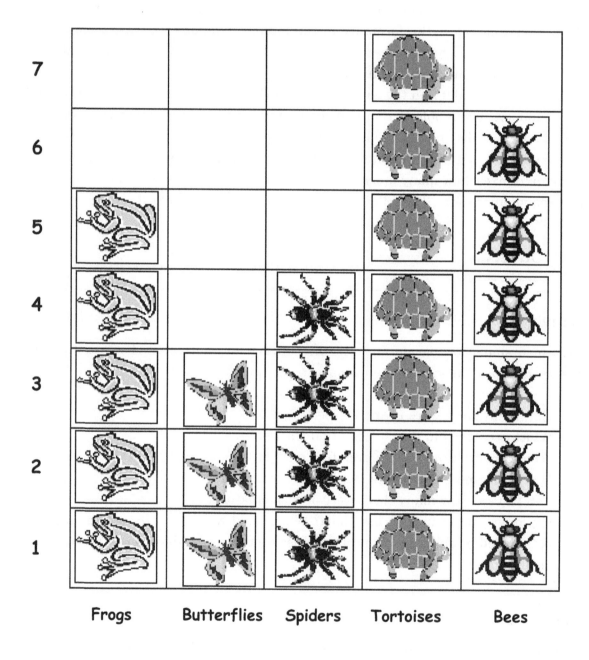

Figure 17.1: Chart to show the numbers of different creatures that children found by a tree in the garden

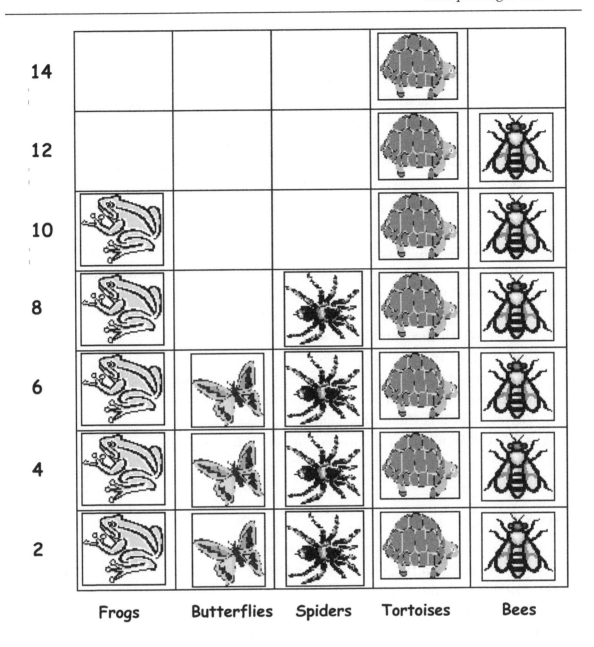

Figure 17.2: Chart to show the numbers of different creatures that children found by a tree in the garden

BAR GRAPHS

This follows on naturally from work with pictograms. However, the concept is more abstract. To help children understand that each step on the scale has the same value, use some of these ideas.

Activity 3

▶ Mark out a grid in the hall, large enough to accommodate the items being used.

▶ Choose a collection of uniform items, which you will have already prepared, e.g. lids from tins of dried milk, shoe box lids, empty drink cans, paper plates, sheets of A5 paper, sheets of A4 paper. (The items chosen represent forms of transport.)

▶ Compare the layout to the pictogram chart. Label the X axis: cars, vans, buses, motorbikes, lorries. Label the Y axis with the numbers 1 to 7.

▶ Choose five children and give each of them a pile of the chosen items. Tell them which column each of them is going to complete.

▶ Give information regarding the number of the various forms of transport passing a certain spot in quarter of an hour. Children lay out their items accordingly.

▶ Ask these questions:
  • How many of each type of vehicle passed the spot?
  • How many vehicles altogether passed the spot?
  • How many more _____ were seen than _____ ?
  • Which type of vehicle was seen the least number of times?
  • Which type of vehicle was seen the most number of times?
  • Why do you think there were more _____ than _____ ?

Let other children lay out the items, changing the numbers.

Ask the children to ask each other questions.

Activity 4

▶ Use the same grid as in Activity 3 and the same items.

▶ Change the scale on the Y axis by numbering the intervals 2, 4, 6, 8, 10, 12, 14. Discuss this with the children.

▶ Choose five children and give each of them a pile of the chosen items. Tell them which column each of them is going to complete.

▶ Give information regarding the number of the various forms of transport passing a certain spot in quarter of an hour. Children lay out their items accordingly. (Be sure to keep to even numbers this time.)

▶ Ask these questions:
  • How many of each type of vehicle passed the spot?
  • How many vehicles altogether passed the spot?
  • How many more _____ were seen than _____ ?
  • Which type of vehicle was seen the least number of times?
  • Which type of vehicle was seen the most number of times?
  • Why do you think there were more _____ than _____ ?

Let other children lay out the items, changing the numbers.

Ask the children to ask each other questions.

Activity 5

This is similar to Activity 4, but this time give odd and even numbers of types of vehicles seen. Children will then have to think of halving their items. This is easier done with A5 and A4 paper than with any of the other suggestions.

Be inventive with activities such as these. It is important that the children are physically involved in constructing the graph.

Activity 6(a)

▶ Make a grid using Excel. This will be your chart. Keep to a 7 × 5 layout as in the above charts, to begin with. These numbers can be varied later.

▶ Mark the X axis with the names of the creatures used in Figure 17.1 and mark the Y axis with the numbers 1 to 7.

▶ Give the children information about the numbers of each creature seen near the tree on a particular day. Ask them to colour in squares to indicate the numbers.

▶ Relabel the Y axis 2, 4, 6, 8, 10, 12, 14. Give numbers of creatures seen and ask children to colour in squares to indicate the numbers.

▶ Vary the names and numbers of creatures to produce different charts.

Activity 6(b)

Use the Excel grid as in Activity 6(a), but this time use it on the computer. Use the fill command to fill in appropriate boxes. (See Figure 17.3.) In this instance no frogs were found.

The details on the X and Y axes can be varied often if you save this grid. Using it several times, keeping the X axis constant and changing the Y axis generates the following questions:

• How do the numbers on the Y axis affect the look of the graph?
• If you change the labels on the intervals, for instance to 5, 10 or 20 units on Y axis, how would this affect the reading of the graph? (See Figure 17.4.)

Older children can start to think about how information is conveyed and how we read tables in newspapers and magazines. They could discuss the importance of reading the axes, of interpretation.

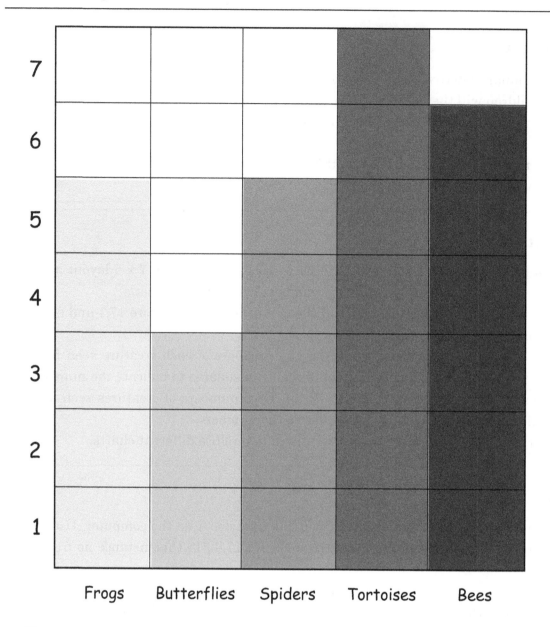

Figure 17.3: Chart to show the numbers of different creatures found by children by a tree in the garden

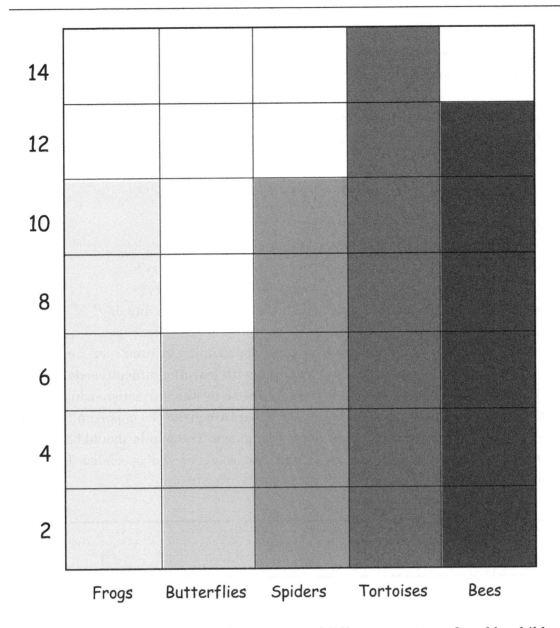

Figure 17.4: Chart to show the numbers of different creatures found by children by a tree in the garden

LINE GRAPHS

Children need to be aware of the variety of graphs that are used in everyday life and to be enabled to make decisions regarding the most appropriate for the purpose in hand. Line graphs can be used to record temperature. The children can record the temperature on each day of the week and plot this on their graph (see Figure 17.5). Do the same and plot over two weeks (see Figure 17.6).

Ask the following questions:

- Which day was the hottest?
- Which day was the coldest?
- How much hotter was the first of these than the second?

- What was the greatest rise from day to day?
- What was the greatest fall from day to day?
- Was the same temperature recorded on any days?

They could choose two or three cities and record their temperatures over a week as reported in the newspaper. Choose cities whose temperatures do not vary too widely. Ask the following questions:

- Which country recorded the hottest day?
- Which country recorded the coldest day?
- How much hotter was the first of these than the second?
- What was the greatest rise from day to day in any one country?
- What was the greatest fall from day to day in any one country?
- Was the same temperature recorded in all three countries on any day?

In both these examples, children are given the opportunity to construct simple line graphs, with help where necessary. Many children with learning difficulties do not find it easy to draw straight lines, so this is a good time to let them practise using a ruler and to emphasise the importance of accuracy. Teachers are given the opportunity to construct a range of questions and use a variety of language. The pupils should be encouraged to think about the language used and use some of the specialist language themselves as appropriate.

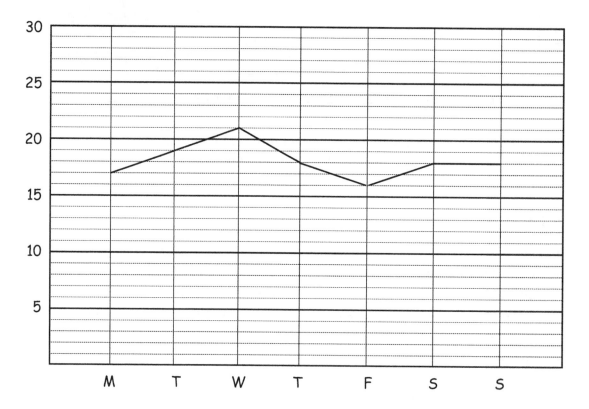

Figure 17.5: Chart to show temperature on each day of the week

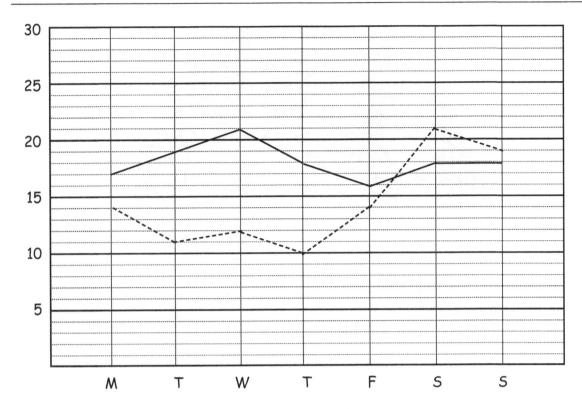

Figure 17.6: Chart to show the temperature on each day of two weeks

PIE CHARTS

To explain these more easily to those children having difficulties, it is important to relate them to something they already understand.

Activity 7

A simple example of a pie chart would be Figure 17.7. This is a chart to show the number of children in a school who either had school lunch, brought their own or went home. Section A is children who have school lunch, B is children who bring a packed lunch and C is children who go home. Most children will see that half have school lunch, a quarter have a packed lunch and a quarter go home for lunch. This is a simple model that relates to concepts already understood. Discuss the importance of the middle of the circle in order to ensure that slices of the pie are accurate.

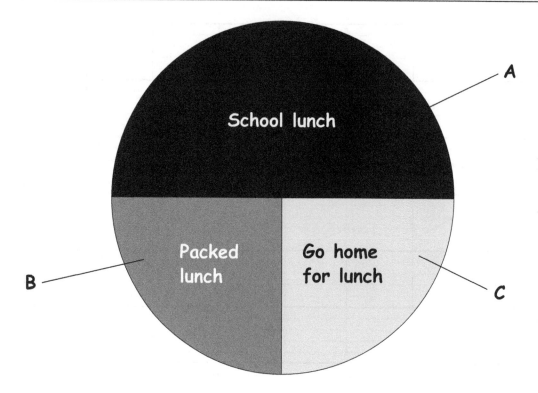

Figure 17.7: Pie chart to show proportions of children taking different kinds of lunch

Activity 8

Make a pie chart marked into ten sections numbered in 10s from 0 to 100 (Figure 17.8). This is a chart to show the colours of the 100 cars that passed the school during one hour yesterday. Demonstrate the following:

- There were 20 red cars.
- There were 10 yellow cars.
- There were 30 silver cars.
- There were 10 black cars.
- There were 20 blue cars.
- There were 10 green cars.

The children should see you drawing lines on the pie chart, from a number on the edge to the centre. You should go round clockwise to demonstrate the above. Draw a line from 0/100 to the centre. Draw another line from 20 to the centre to show the number of red cars seen. Colour in the segment. Discuss this to ensure that all children are clear.

Ask children to suggest where you should draw the next line to show 10 yellow cars. Continue in this fashion. In this example you can use the actual car colours to fill in the segments. You are now ready to demonstrate how quickly you can see facts on a pie chart. Ask the following questions:

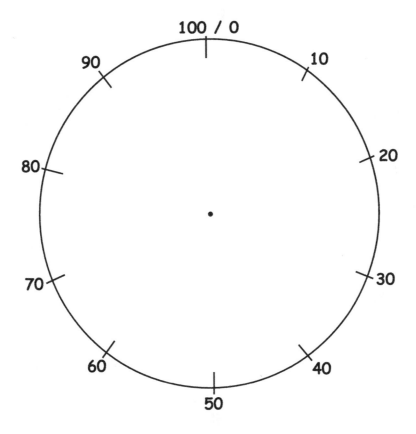

Figure 17.8

- Which colour car passed most often?
- Which colours passed the same number of times?
- How many more red cars than yellow ones passed?
- How can you check that you have included all the 100 cars?
- Do you think the segments could be arranged in any other way?

Give out copies of the chart and ask the children to cut it into slices. Now ask them to rearrange the slices. Can they still answer the above questions? Be inventive. Ask the children to ask each other questions. Questions they put may include: 'Why have you arranged your slices differently from mine?' 'Why did we see so many silver cars?' 'Why are three slices the same size?'

Activity 9

Mark the pie chart like a clock, in 5s from 0 to 60 (Figure 17.9). This is a chart to show the favourite European holiday destinations of 60 people. Demonstrate the following:

- 15 people like going to France.
- 20 people like going to Spain.
- 15 people like going to Italy.

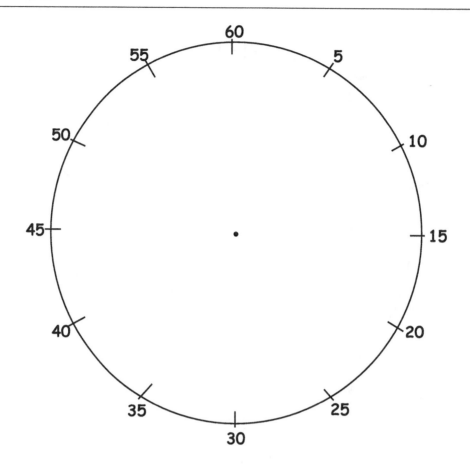

Figure 17.9

- 5 people like going to Germany.
- 5 people like going to Holland.

You can choose any destinations you like. Include more if you want to, although these quantities are easier to deal with at first. Choose cities in England.

Now demonstrate the use of this chart. Draw a line from 60/0 to the centre. Draw another line from 15 to the centre to show the number of people who like to go to France. Colour in the segment. Discuss this to ensure that all children are clear.

Ask children to suggest where you should draw the next line to show 20 people who prefer to go to Spain. Continue in this fashion. Ask the following questions:

- What is the favourite holiday destination?
- What comes next?
- Which are the least popular destinations?
- How many more people prefer France to Holland?
- How many prefer France and Italy?
- How many do not prefer France and Italy?
- How can you check that you have included all the 60 people?
- Do you think the segments could be arranged in any other way?

Give out copies of the chart and ask the children to cut it into slices. Now ask them to rearrange the slices. Can they still answer the above questions? Be inventive. Ask the children to ask each other questions.

In this example you should relate the numbers to the clock. You can then see that a quarter of the people prefer France and a quarter prefer Italy. That means that half prefer France or Italy.

RESOURCES

- Pictogram
- Collection of uniform items
- A5 and A4 paper
- Labels
- Scissors
- Printed grids
- Rulers
- Graph paper

18 Probability

The Numeracy Strategy has examples of activities in probability, which are practical and clear enough for use with most pupils. Children who find number work difficult to do at speed may well find other aspects of mathematics much easier to understand.

Some children will spend a long time on one activity and may not have the variety of experiences that other children have. However, for the child with learning difficulties, quality, supported time with one item will help more than being pushed on to try something else.

Parents can help by making up games and activities. Use horse-racing meetings to look at the odds. Have guessing games to predict what is going to happen next, ensuring that suitable prizes are at hand.

At home and at school, children can practise mental arithmetic and multiplication tables by finding the mean of sets of numbers. For example, to find the mean of 8, 4, 12, 11 and 10, children add the numbers and divide the total (45) by 5.

Explain the language. For example, relate 'mode' to fashion. Go shopping and ask which is the most popular item being sold. Find out what is the most popular food being bought in a burger bar and a pizza restaurant.

To understand chance, whether statements or events can be classified as certain, likely, unlikely or impossible, ask the children to make up statements themselves. Each child should try to find one statement to fit each classification. Write the statements on paper (word processing would be best) and mix them up. Then, as a group or class the children can try to fit them to the correct categories.

We have found that our children enjoy working with dice and the examples quoted in the National Numeracy Strategy are helpful for them.

The language of probability is not easy to remember by children with mathematical learning difficulties. Teachers must remember how much this language needs to be rehearsed and how important the concept is.

Probability can be left out, or squeezed into a short period of time, due to pressure of time. We have found that the children need a lot of help to understand and use the probability scale, and it is this that needs the most attention.

19 Special Project: Time Travel

This is a project that a teacher planned for her group of Year 5 children who found maths very difficult. They were studying the planets as part of their science work and the teacher decided to develop this cross-curricular theme as an attempt to get them to see the connections between maths and other areas of the curriculum. It was hoped that they would gain a feel for mathematics while using their imaginations and having fun.

During their journey through the solar system they found out about:

- circles and ellipses (the solar system);
- cylinders and cones (rockets);
- time;
- fractions;
- money;
- addition and subtraction.

Activity 1

► Give the children a plan of the solar system, with the (invented) time given to travel between each planet (see Photocopiable Sheet M).

► Ask the children to make a rocket to go into space. They must plan their nets to make cylinders and cones. The net of a 3D shape is the 2D plan that can be folded to make the 3D shape, e.g. net of a cube could look like this:

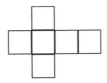

This is not an easy exercise for many children, especially the dyslexic or dyspraxic ones. Accuracy needs to be emphasised when measuring and cutting out. How many cylinders and cones do they see in their everyday life?

Activity 2

Ask the children to draw a map of the solar system using circles and ellipses and considering scale. This will need a lot of teacher input, but the children will learn a lot about map-making and scale. Teachers monitoring this exercise can decide how accurate they want to be. For many children with learning difficulties the understanding of relative differences in size and scale is sufficient; they do not need to be totally accurate.

Activity 3

▶ Ask children to plan a journey from Earth into space, deciding where you want to go first. For instance, it will take five hours to reach Mars, and if you were then to go to Saturn it would take five-and-a-half hours plus 17 hours. Teachers can invent many exercises based on this. Children can travel to a variety of planets.

▶ Children can list the journeys taken and compare the times taken. They can talk about difference, less than, more than. In the example given, whole and half-hours only have been given. Teachers can include quarter-hours also. Can the children work out how many minutes each journey would take?

▶ Give the children empty diary pages for the month in which the work is being done and the month following. Ask them to plot their journey on these pages, noting the day and time they leave Earth and when they arrive at their respective destinations. This gives them the opportunity to think about time facts (number of hours in the day) and to use, if appropriate, the 24-hour clock.

Activity 4

▶ Ask children to make a travel ticket. How much will it cost? Compare the cost of travelling to other destinations in the world. Look up ticket prices on the Internet or in brochures. How much more expensive will it be to go to some places than others?

This can lead to a discussion of what else you could buy for the amount of the ticket.

RESOURCES

- Plans of solar system
- Paper
- Compasses
- Pages from a diary
- Travel tickets
- Travel brochures

Time Travel

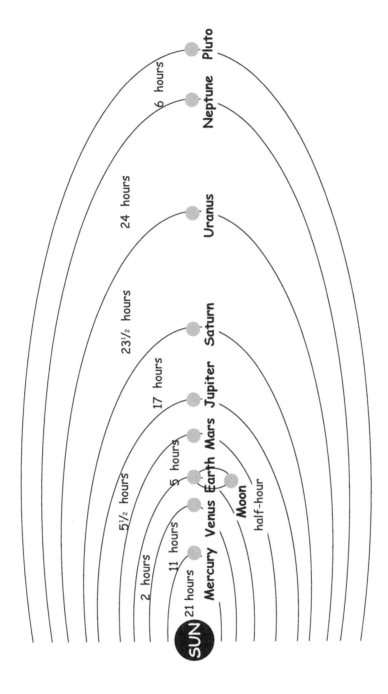

SUN

21 hours — Mercury

2 hours — Venus

11 hours — Earth

half-hour — Moon

5 hours — Mars

5½ hours — Jupiter

17 hours — Saturn

23½ hours — Uranus

24 hours — Neptune

6 hours — Pluto

Photocopiable Sheet M

For Product Safety Concerns and Information please contact our EU
representative GPSR@taylorandfrancis.com Taylor & Francis Verlag GmbH,
Kaufingerstraße 24, 80331 München, Germany

Printed and bound by CPI Group (UK) Ltd, Croydon, CR0 4YY
08/06/2025
01896981-0013